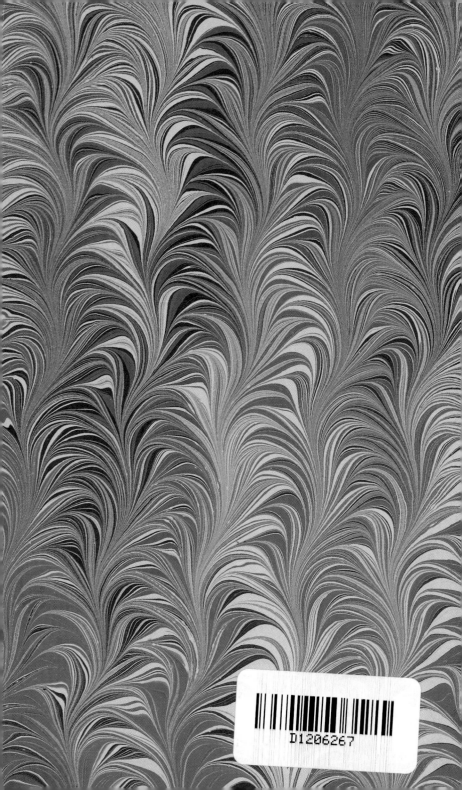

The
Ten Commandments of Typography

The
Ten Commandments of Typography

Paul Felton

MERRELL
LONDON · NEW YORK

Acknowledgements

I should like to thank my university tutor, Andy Ellison, my parents, Sandra and Roy, my nan, Doreen, and my girlfriend, Beki.
Thanks to Jonathan for the foreword, and to all the friends, family and designers who have helped make this book possible.

Fonts used in *The Ten Commandments of Typography*:

Amazone

Bauer Bodoni Bold

gilcimar *Gilcimar*

Janus Moire

𝕷inotext

Metroline *Metroline*

signal

Stempel Garamond Roman, *Italic,* **Bold**

Tyrnavia Regular, Xperts

Univers 47 Condensed Light

Velocity *Velocity*

Weird *Weird*

❧ Woodtype Ornaments 2 ☙

First published 2006 by Merrell Publishers Limited

Head office
81 Southwark Street
London SE1 0HX

New York office
740 Broadway, 12th Floor
New York, NY 10003

merrellpublishers.com

British Library Cataloguing-in-Publication data:
Felton, Paul
The ten commandments of typography ; Type heresy :
breaking the ten commandments of typography
1.Type and type-founding 2.Graphic design (Typography)
I.Title II.Felton, Paul. Type heresy
686.2'2

ISBN-13: 978-1-8589-4355-8
ISBN-10: 1-8589-4355-8

Produced by Merrell Publishers Limited
Designed by Paul Felton
Copy-edited by Richard Dawes

Printed and bound in Slovenia

Contents

Preface

The
Ten Commandments of Typography

The Commandments are a rock where you can find safety. When designing, call on the mighty laws and you shall be delivered from any problems. When the bonds of Barnbrook tighten around you, or the snares of Carson are set to catch you, remember the Lord's words: "Happy is the man who does not take the wicked for his guide, nor walk the road that sinners tread." Why are designers in turmoil? Why do typographers hatch their evil plots? The modern kings of graphic design, Frost, Keedy and VanderLans, stand ready and conspire together against the Lord and His rules. "Let us break their fetters!" they cry. "Let us disregard legibility!" But when judgement comes on their work, the wicked will not stand firm. The Lord watches over the world of design and typography and guides the way of the righteous, but the way of the wicked is for ever doomed.

God speaks thus to the wicked typographers:

"What right have you to recite my rules
and make so free with the words of my holy alphabet,
you who hate correction
and turn your back on my laws when designing?
If you meet illegibility, you choose it as your friend,
you make common cause with the unstructured,
you charge your design with chaos
and harness your type to disarray.
You are forever thinking against the rules,
stabbing the very constitution in the back.
But pixel by pixel I will rebuke your design to your face.
Think on this, you who forget God and His mighty laws."

Introduction

The
Ten Commandments of Typography

IN THE BEGINNING God created type. And the world was without form, and void, and darkness was upon the face of legibility. God said, "Let there be ten rules to govern the use of type", and there came structure, order and legibility, and God saw that this was good. But type could not exist without man, so God created man. From His race of men He chose twelve of the worthy to be His type disciples and to spread the laws of typography to others. The Lord then spoke to His disciples and gave them the ten rules by which every typographer must abide, to gain passage to type Heaven. The laws helped typographers and designers produce endless amounts of beautiful work. They became known as *The Ten Commandments of Typography*.

Matthew Carter

On Typography

How important do you think the main typographic 'rules' are, and should they always be followed?

The advantage of rules is that they can prevent mistakes; the disadvantage is that they can prevent discoveries. When I started work in a type foundry fifty years ago my efforts as a learner consisted entirely of mistakes. This was pretty discouraging, but an experienced workman told me, "Always look carefully at a mistake before you discard it – it might be better than what you intended". I think there's more to the design process than simple trial and error, but errors are often the price paid for successful trials, and rules learned by rote are valuable only if they are constantly questioned.

As someone who is predominantly a type designer, are you often saddened to see your typefaces used in the wrong context or applied badly?

I may be more forgiving about this than many type designers: I reckon I might as well accept what I can't police. Overall, the experience of seeing my typefaces in use has been a good and encouraging one, but there are obviously examples from time to time of a typeface being put in a situation where it has to fail, and that's annoying. On the other hand, type designers learn from seeing their work in use out there in the world. When a typeface is put through its paces in exactly the way its designer intended, that can be very rewarding, but it's not particularly informative. Seeing it used in an unexpected way – good or bad – can be a much more revealing lesson.

From an email to Paul Felton

The Twelve Disciples of Typography

Herbert Bayer

1900–1985, Austria
Graphic designer and type designer
Work includes: German banknotes; *Die Neue Linie* magazine; Universal typeface

Derek Birdsall

1934–, United Kingdom
Graphic designer and writer
Work includes: *Common Worship*; *Notes on Book Design*; Penguin Books

Matthew Carter

1937–, United Kingdom
Type designer and writer, founded Bitstream
Work includes: Bell Centennial, Georgia, Shelley Script and Verdana typefaces

Lazar El Lissitzky

1890–1941, Russia
Graphic designer, painter and writer
Work includes: *From Two Quadrants*; propaganda poster *Beat the Whites with the Red Wedge*

Adrian Frutiger

1928–, Switzerland
Type designer, associated with Deberney & Peignot, and Linotype
Work includes: Univers and Frutiger typefaces

Eric Gill

1882–1940, United Kingdom
Type designer, sculptor, carver, printmaker and writer
Work includes: *Essay on Typography*; Gill Sans and Perpetua typefaces

The Twelve Disciples of Typography

Jonathan Hoefler

1970–, United States of America
Type designer, founded Hoefler Type Foundry
Work includes: Hoefler Text, Didot HTF and Pavisse typefaces

László Moholy-Nagy

1895–1946, Hungary
Graphic designer, sculptor, photographer and writer
Work includes: *Malerei Fotografie Film*

Josef Müller-Brockmann

1914–1996, Switzerland
Graphic designer and writer
 Work includes: *The Graphic Artist and his Design Problems*; Zurich Tonhalle posters

Paul Renner

1878–1956, Germany
Graphic designer, type designer, painter and writer
Work includes: Futura typeface; *Typographie als Kunst*

Erik Spiekermann

1947–, Germany
Graphic designer, type designer and writer, founded Meta Design and FontShop
Work includes: *Stop Stealing Sheep*; Meta, Officina and Info typefaces

Jan Tschichold

1902–1974, Germany
Graphic designer, type designer and writer
Work includes: Munich film posters; *Die Neue Typographie*; Penguin Books; Sabon typeface

The
Ten Commandments of Typography

Hear the word of thy Lord God:

I. Thou shalt not apply more than three typefaces in a document.

Always remember that simplicity reigns over
the disarray and confusion that the use of
many typefaces causes.

In the beginning God created type.

HEADLINE – BAUER BODONI BOLD, 14PT

And the world was without form, and void.

SUBHEADER – AMAZONE, 11PT

And darkness was upon the face of legibility. God said, "Let there be ten rules to govern the use of type", and there came structure, order and legibility, and God saw that this was good.

BODY TEXT – STEMPEL GARAMOND ROMAN, 8PT

Hear the word of thy Lord God:

II. Thou shalt lay headlines large and at the top of a page.

Raise the headline to a windy height, roar out your
summons, and beckon with considerable type size.

In the beginning
God created type

HEADLINE – BAUER BODONI BOLD, 20PT AND 26PT

In the beginning God created type. And the world was without form, and void, and darkness was upon the face of legibility. God said, "Let there be ten rules to govern the use of type", and there came structure, order and legibility, and God saw that this was good.

BODY TEXT – STEMPEL GARAMOND ROMAN, 8PT

3

Hear the word of thy Lord God:

III. Thou shalt employ no other type size than 8pt to 10pt for body copy.

The Lord will not leave unpunished
he who disregards this rule.

In the beginning God created type. And the world was without form,
and void, and darkness was upon the face of legibility. God said,
"Let there be ten rules to govern the use of type", and there came
structure, order and legibility, and God saw that this was good.

STEMPEL GARAMOND ROMAN, 8PT WITH 11PT LEADING

In the beginning God created type. And the world was
without form, and void, and darkness was upon the face of
legibility. God said, "Let there be ten rules to govern the use
of type", and there came structure, order and legibility, and
God saw that this was good.

STEMPEL GARAMOND ROMAN, 9PT WITH 12PT LEADING

In the beginning God created type. And the world was
without form, and void, and darkness was upon the face
of legibility. God said, "Let there be ten rules to govern
the use of type", and there came structure, order and
legibility, and God saw that this was good.

STEMPEL GARAMOND ROMAN, 10PT WITH 13PT LEADING

4

Hear the word of thy Lord God:

IV. Remember that a typeface that is not legible is not truly a typeface.

The dingbats and the disordered fuse fonts that
foundries hold sacred are all worthless, and cursed
are all who make them their delight.

.

In the beginning god created type, and the world was without form, and void.

GILCIMAR

In the beginning god created type, and the world was without form, and void.

JANUS MOIRE

In the beginning god created type. And the world was without form, and void.

METROLINE

In the beginning god created type, and the world was without form, and void.

SIGNAL

In the beginning God created type. And the world was without form, and void.

VELOCITY

In the beginning god created type. And the world was without form, and void.

WEIRD-TOO NEGATIVE

Hear the word of thy Lord God:

V. Honour thy kerning, so that white space becomes visually equalized between characters.

Kerning will save the reader time
in deciphering writings.

Ye Av ot

WITHOUT KERNING

Ye Av ot

WITH KERNING

in the beginning

NORMAL TRACKING

in the beginning

LOOSE TRACKING

in the beginning

TIGHT TRACKING

Hear the word of thy Lord God:

VI. Thou shalt lay stress discreetly upon elements within text.

The glory of God is to keep things hidden,
but the glory of the foolish typographer is to
over-emphasize them.

In the beginning God created type. And the world was without form, and void, and darkness was upon the face of legibility. God said, *"Let there be ten rules to govern the use of type"*, and there came structure, order and legibility, and God saw that this was good.

ITALICS

In the beginning God created type. And the world was without form, and void, and darkness was upon the face of legibility. God said, "<u>Let there be ten rules to govern the use of type</u>", and there came structure, order and legibility, and God saw that this was good.

UNDERLINING

In the beginning God created type. And the world was without form, and void, and darkness was upon the face of legibility. God said, "Let there be ten rules to govern the use of type", and there came structure, order and legibility, and God saw that this was good.

COLOUR

In the beginning God created type. And the world was without form, and void, and darkness was upon the face of legibility. God said, **"Let there be ten rules to govern the use of type"**, and there came structure, order and legibility, and God saw that this was good.

FONT WEIGHT

Hear the word of thy Lord God:

VII. Thou shalt not use only capitals when setting vast body copy.

Let thine eyes be fixed on the ascenders,
bowls and finials of lowercase type.

In the beginning God created type. And the world was without form, and void, and darkness was upon the face of legibility. God said, "Let there be ten rules to govern the use of type", and there came structure, order and legibility, and God saw that this was good.

UPPERCASE AND LOWERCASE TEXT

IN THE BEGINNING GOD CREATED TYPE. AND THE WORLD WAS WITHOUT FORM, AND VOID, AND DARKNESS WAS UPON THE FACE OF LEGIBILITY. GOD SAID, "LET THERE BE TEN RULES TO GOVERN THE USE OF TYPE", AND THERE CAME STRUCTURE, ORDER AND LEGIBILITY, AND GOD SAW THAT THIS WAS GOOD.

UPPERCASE TEXT

8

Hear the word of thy Lord God:

VIII. Thou shalt always align letters and words on a baseline.

The Lord designed letterforms to coexist side by side on an invisible line, so thou shalt give them a straight path to follow.

In the beginning God created type.

WORD DEVIATION

I n t h e b e g i n n i g G o d c r e a t e d t y p e

LETTER DEVIATION

I   G
n   o
          d

t   c
h   r
e   e
          a
b   t
e   e
g   d
i
n
n   t
i   y
n   p
g   e

VERTICAL DEVIATION

9

Hear the word of thy Lord God:

IX. Thou shalt use flush-left, ragged-right type alignment.

Renounce the use of other alignments, for they
bring extra torment upon already busy eyes.

In the beginning God created type. And the world was without form, and void, and darkness was upon the face of legibility. God said, "Let there be ten rules to govern the use of type", and there came structure, order and legibility.

FLUSH-LEFT, RAGGED-RIGHT TEXT

In the beginning God created type. And the world was without form, and void, and darkness was upon the face of legibility. God said, "Let there be ten rules to govern the use of type", and there came structure, order and legibility.

FLUSH-RIGHT, RAGGED-LEFT TEXT

In the beginning God created type. And the world was without form, and void, and darkness was upon the face of legibility. God said, "Let there be ten rules to govern the use of type", and there came structure, order and legibility.

JUSTIFIED TEXT

In the beginning God created type. And the world was without form, and void, and darkness was upon the face of legibility. God said, "Let there be ten rules to govern the use of type", and there came structure, order and legibility.

CENTRED TEXT

Hear the word of thy Lord God:

X. Thou shalt not make lines too short or too long.

I command you to trust in an utmost of
seventy characters per line, while a minimum
of forty shall suffice.

In the beginning
God created
type. And the
world was
without form,
and void, and
darkness was
upon the face of
legibility. God
said, "Let there
be ten rules to
govern the use
of type", and
there came
structure, order
and legibility.

SHORT LINES

In the beginning God created type. And the world was
without form, and void, and darkness was upon the face
of legibility. God said, "Let there be ten rules to govern the
use of type", and there came structure, order and legibility.

MEDIUM LINES

In the beginning God created type. And the world was without form, and void, and
darkness was upon the face of legibility. God said, "Let there be ten rules to govern the
use of type", and there came structure, order and legibility.

LONG LINES

typographic heaven

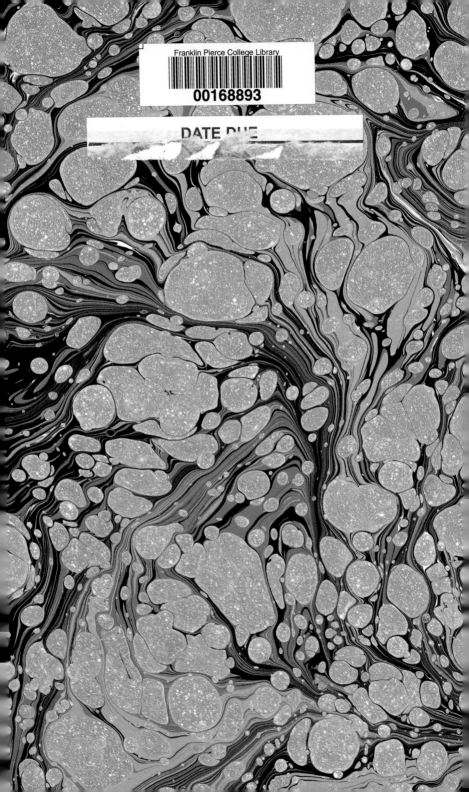

Type Heresy

Type Heresy

Paul Felton

Foreword by Jonathan Barnbrook

MERRELL
LONDON · NEW YORK

Fonts used in *Type Heresy*

Type Heresy

JONATHAN
BARNBROOK

IN THE COURSE OF MY WORKING LIFE MANY STUDENTS HAVE ASKED ME HOW THEY CAN LEARN MORE ABOUT 'PROPER' TYPOGRAPHY.

It reminds me of the mantra that my tutors would trot out regularly: "Learn the rules of typography before you break them!" they would say with grim expressions on their faces, reminiscent of prison-camp guards. I always suspected that this was more about stopping us students having fun because of the God-awful work they were forced to do now they were 'old', than a truthful statement about good typography. Finally, though, ready to learn, I asked the aforementioned tutors in my loudest voice,

"TEACH ME THE RULES",
"PLEASE, I WANT TO LEARN THE RULES", and again
"I AM EAGER TO KNOW THE GODDAMN RULES, JUST SIT ME DOWN AND TELL THEM TO ME!"

but would they? No, they bloody well wouldn't. Of course, then I realized that most of them didn't actually know 'the rules' themselves. It was just a well-meaning statement. Most found the subject too dry and complex either to learn or to teach.

CONTINUED ...

SURELY, THEN, THERE SHOULD BE A DIFFERENT

APPROACH TO LEARNING ABOUT TYPOGRAPHY?

Hmm ... Unfortunately there is no escaping the fact that the basic rules are dry, and the only real way to learn them is to get a proper mentor or sit down and progress painfully through them yourself. With a bit of extra reading around the subject, however, and by bringing your own interests into it, you will find that typography truly reflects the whole of human life, and those rules of punctuation, leading and so on are directly linked to language, with all its complexities of double meanings, intonations and so on. You will eventually find that it is a direct visual representation of the tone of voice with which we express the spirit of our time.

Typography, dare I say it, can even sometimes be rather ... funny, which is where this book comes in. Paul Felton has written something quite rare – a book about typography that is both informative and entertaining.

PREFACE

Satan is the adversary of God. Thus, Satan is typographic evil personified. Followers of the Ten Commandments consider Satan to be a real being, created by God. Satan and the other spirits who followed him rebelled against God's Commandments and were cast out of Heaven by their Creator. Satan, or the devil as he is often called, was allowed to set up his own design kingdom in Hell and to send out Fallen Angels to prowl the earth for converts to the dark side of typography. The demonic world seems to have been allowed to exist for one purpose only: to tempt humans to turn away from God's rules. Many believe that Satan can 'possess' designers. Possession is bodily invasion by the devil, who forces a designer to break the rules of typographic design. One of the more interesting aspects of Satanism is the recurrent theme of designers making a pact with the devil. The best known of such stories is that Satan will bestow design accolades and awards upon one for a limited time, in exchange for possession of one's soul.

TO HELL

WITH THE RULES!

We propose a revolution in typography. Satan and his
Fallen Angels are renouncing the sacred Commandments.
The typography of the disciples is dull, rigid, linear, well-
tempered design using extremely unexpressive sans-serif
letterforms. We reject the authoritarian voices of the
disciples, who preach a single reading; there is hardly
any interaction between the message and the reader.
Rick Poyner says:

Introduction

"The aim is to promote multiple, rather than fixed,
readings, to provoke the reader into becoming an
active participant in the construction of the
message. Later Modernist typography sought to
reduce complexity, and to clarify content, but the
new typographers relish ambiguity ... ."

We are very
reluctant to
accept that the Commandments are the only way to design
and that they are inscribed on tablets of stone.

We are here to show the light to designers who are bored by the dull solutions and
rigid perfection that the Commandments offer. Fallen Angel Barry Deck says:
"I am really interested in typography that isn't perfect, type that reflects more truly the
imperfect language of an imperfect world, inhabited by imperfect beings."
People who cherish the Commandments are stuck with traditional,
uninteresting design solutions. According to one of the antichrists, Phil Baines,
"Legibility presents information as facts rather than as an experience." He believes that logic
and linearity can sometimes be OK, but that they satisfy only the rational side of the brain.
For Poyner and the Fallen Angels,
"Typography should address our capacity for intuitive insight and simultaneous perception,
and stimulate our senses as well as engaging our intellect."
So let the day of the Commandments be in the past. Let's get our audience involved
in our design as much as we typographers are. Help us create Armageddon for the
Ten Commandments and let all hell break loose!

JEFFERY KEEDY

How important are the Ten Commandments of Typography, and must we rigidly abide by them?

The first thing one learns about typography and type design is that there are many rules and maxims that enlighten the neophyte. The second is that such rules are made to be broken. And the third is that 'breaking the rules' has always been just another one of the rules.

How has the emergence of rule-breaking typography changed the way a viewer interacts with a piece of work?

Deliberate, wilful rule-breaking is done for the desired effect of getting the viewer's attention. It works – that's why people do it. But some people break the rules simply because they don't know them. It is important to remember that 'rule-breaking' predates 'rule-making' by quite a few years. In the history of typography, very little of what has been produced follows the rules, but this may change as many of the rules will be incorporated into our software. Then people will be following rules that they aren't even aware of. Is this progress?

One of the Commandments states that you should not apply more than three typefaces in a document. What are your views on this?

Simple methodologies generate simple results. Complex methodologies generate complex results. The idea that it is "really difficult to do something simple very well" is a load of Modernist propaganda (crap), but will always be very popular with lazy and unimaginative designers. But, most importantly, simple is fast, and designers are expected to work ridiculously fast nowadays, so it is no wonder that they have made the good old clean and simple Modernism fashionable (again). Now it seems that even designers themselves believe that design is not worth investing time in. Go to the Victoria and Albert Museum in London and look at the design of the nineteenth century. It takes time to do that kind of work. New technology is supposed to give us more time for what is important, but it seems to have taken it away from designers. Too bad for us.

FROM AN EMAIL TO PAUL FELTON

Satan and his Fallen Angels of Typography

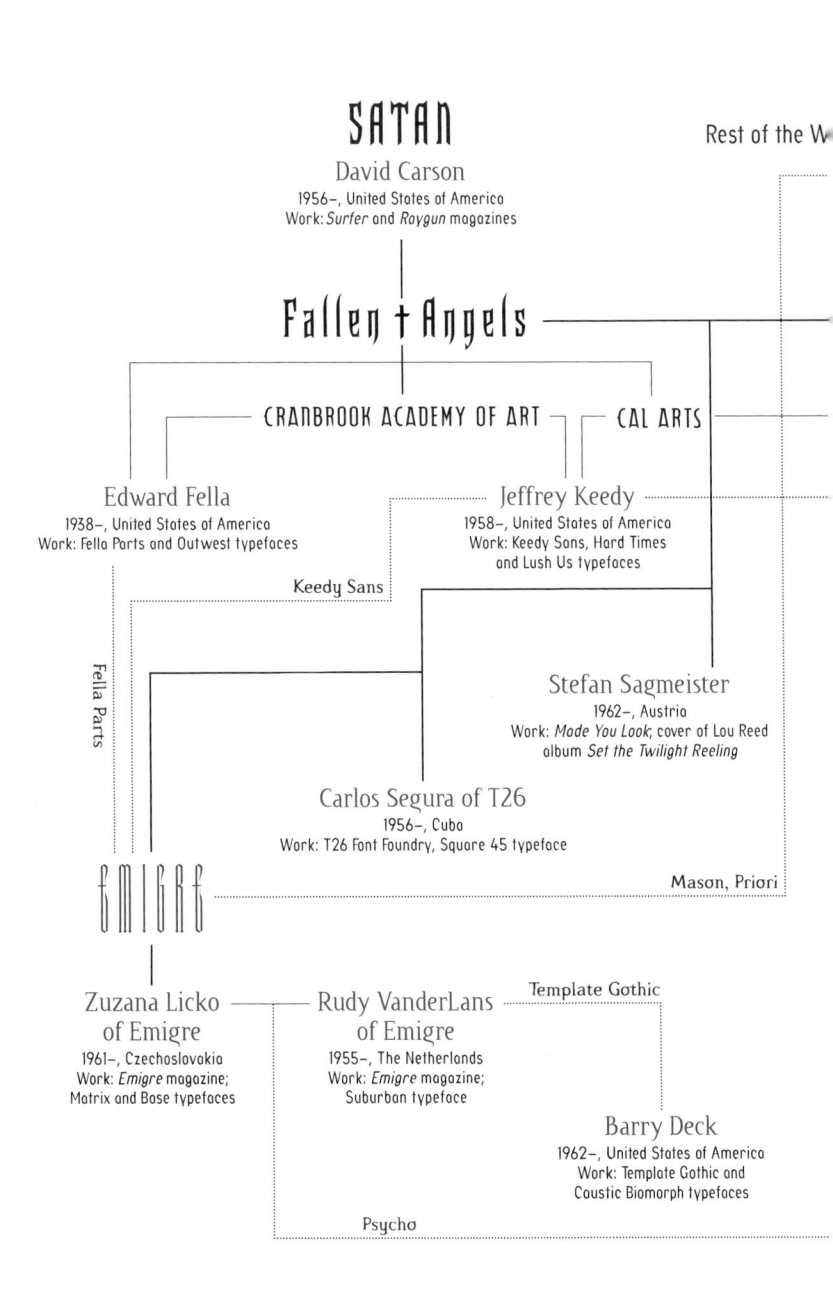

SATAN
David Carson
1956–, United States of America
Work: *Surfer* and *Raygun* magazines

Rest of the W

Fallen † Angels

CRANBROOK ACADEMY OF ART — CAL ARTS

Edward Fella
1938–, United States of America
Work: Fella Parts and Outwest typefaces

Jeffrey Keedy
1958–, United States of America
Work: Keedy Sans, Hard Times
and Lush Us typefaces

Keedy Sans

Fella Parts

Stefan Sagmeister
1962–, Austria
Work: *Made You Look*; cover of Lou Reed
album *Set the Twilight Reeling*

Carlos Segura of T26
1956–, Cuba
Work: T26 Font Foundry, Square 45 typeface

EMIGRE

Mason, Priori

Zuzana Licko
of Emigre
1961–, Czechoslovakia
Work: *Emigre* magazine;
Matrix and Base typefaces

Rudy VanderLans
of Emigre
1955–, The Netherlands
Work: *Emigre* magazine;
Suburban typeface

Template Gothic

Barry Deck
1962–, United States of America
Work: Template Gothic and
Caustic Biomorph typefaces

Psycho

Satan and his Fallen Angels were once among the angelic typographic few.
Now they have been cast out of God's Kingdom. Below are the principal Fallen Angels.

United Kingdom

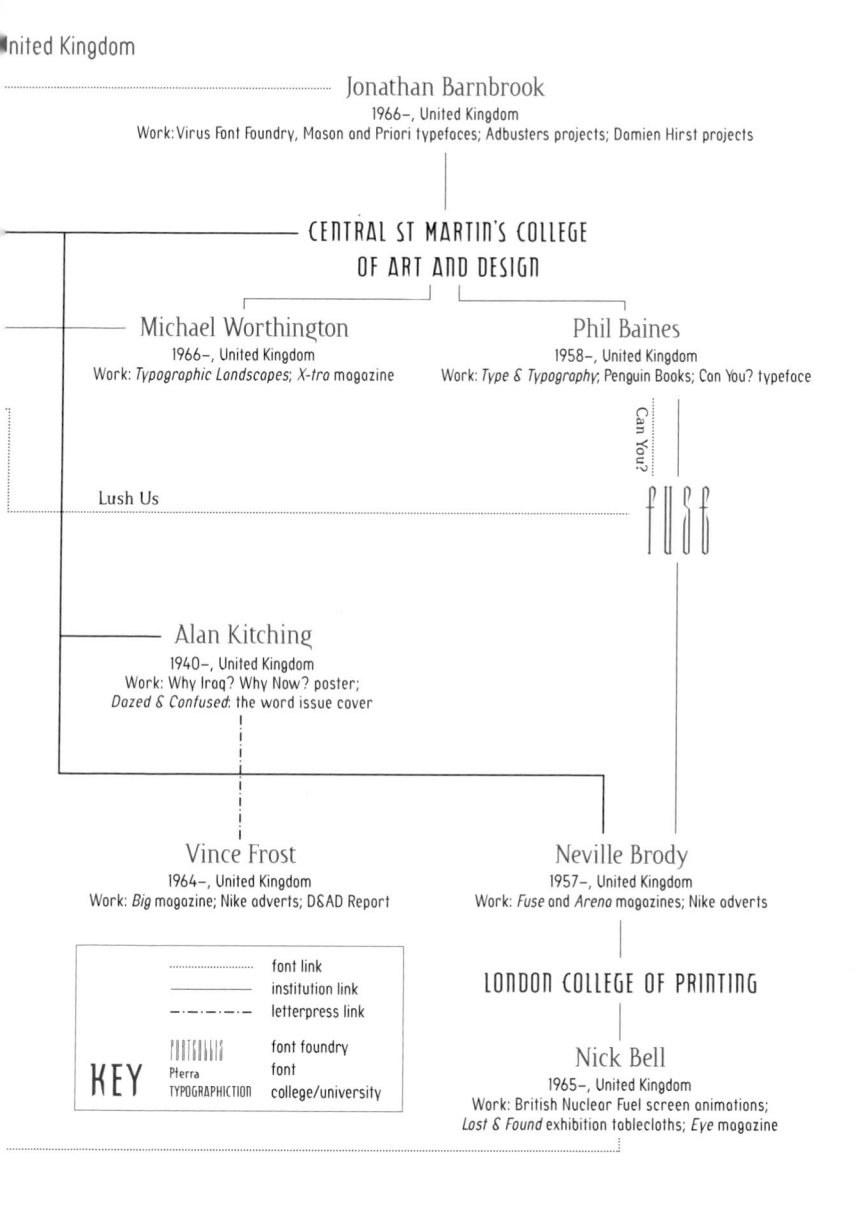

Jonathan Barnbrook
1966–, United Kingdom
Work: Virus Font Foundry, Mason and Priori typefaces; Adbusters projects; Damien Hirst projects

CENTRAL ST MARTIN'S COLLEGE
OF ART AND DESIGN

Michael Worthington
1966–, United Kingdom
Work: *Typographic Landscapes*; *X-tra* magazine

Phil Baines
1958–, United Kingdom
Work: *Type & Typography*; Penguin Books; Can You? typeface

Can You?

Lush Us

FUSE

Alan Kitching
1940–, United Kingdom
Work: Why Iraq? Why Now? poster;
Dazed & Confused: the word issue cover

Vince Frost
1964–, United Kingdom
Work: *Big* magazine; Nike adverts; D&AD Report

Neville Brody
1957–, United Kingdom
Work: *Fuse* and *Arena* magazines; Nike adverts

LONDON COLLEGE OF PRINTING

Nick Bell
1965–, United Kingdom
Work: British Nuclear Fuel screen animations;
Lost & Found exhibition tablecloths; *Eye* magazine

KEY

··············	font link
————	institution link
–·–·–·–	letterpress link
FONTFOUNDRY	font foundry
Pterra	font
TYPOGRAPHICTION	college/university

19

Type Heresy

Breaking the Ten Commandments of Typography

Thou shalt not apply more than three typefaces in a document.

Break the fetters imposed by the use of only three typefaces. The Lord giveth fonts and has instructed us not to be wasteful, so use as many as you desire!

1

THOU SHALT APPLY AS MANY DIFFERENT TYPEFACES AS THOU WANTETH TO! WOULDN'T THE WORLD BE INCREDIBLY BLOODY BORING IF ALL WE USED WAS ONE FONT FOR HEADLINES ANOTHER FOR SUBHEADERS AND FINALLY ONE MORE TO SET ALL YOUR BODY COPY IN. IT DOESN'T GIVE YOU MUCH SCOPE TO BE VERY CREATIVE WITH YOUR WORK, DOES IT? THE LORD GIVETH FONTS SO LET US USE THEM BEFORE HE TAKETH THEM AWAY.

2

Thou shalt lay headlines large and at the top of a page.

Let thine eyes be seduced by the hierarchy of type.
Bolder fonts, even at the same size as body copy,
will attract the eye first.

What did you read first? For God's sake, don't say you read the headline first! How the hell has that happened? I thought headlines had to go at the top of the page and be huge in order to work? Here it is in 10pt, the recommended size for body copy according to the Ten Commandments, and placed at the bottom of a page, but you still read it first?

or here ...

Christ! I don't know what to say! It just goes to show that headlines can be put anywhere and at any size and still work. Anyway, who says that you have to read them first on every article? God help us if every designer stuck to this rule. Imagine what magazines would look like. Drab, I think the word is. Your copy of *Baseline* would look identical to *Heat*!

or here!

or here ...

God forbid
we put it down here and fairly small

3

Thou shalt employ no other type size than 8pt to 10pt for body copy.

Do not forsake smaller or bigger sizes, for they can make a plain text document look wickedly sensuous.

For Heaven's sake! Why? Body copy is still legible and readable at this size and

at this size as well. If you were competing in a speed-reading competition maybe it would be best to abide by the Commandments, but let's face it, that's not going to happen. So stop boring your readers to death and give them some visual excitement.

4

Remember that a typeface that is not legible is not truly a typeface.

Be seduced into trying new and expressive typefaces and break free from the security of traditional fonts.

The black area you can see is part
of a Garamond 'g'. But you can't read
that it is a 'g', so it is not legible.
If the Commandments are to
be adhered to, in this instance is
Garamond no longer a typeface?

Janus Moire, by contrast, is not
strictly legible, but it portrays a sense
of mazed letterforms, so it does
communicate as a typeface:

"It is the reader's familiarity with
faces that accounts for their legibility."

Rick Poyner

"We might find it impossible to read
'Blackletter' with ease today, but in
pre-war Germany it was the
dominant letterform."

Zuzana Licko of Emigre

5

Honour thy kerning, so that white space becomes visually equalized between characters.

Treat kerning with total irreverence and expose the devious space between letterforms.

y
t
h
g
i
m
t
s

c hr i st

Letterforms can be sly and deceitful, and certain combinations of characters will have cumbersome spaces between them. Words that are not kerned can suggest an amateur typographer; but words that have had their kerning and tracking deliberately exaggerated can look devilishly good, as Satan himself, David Carson, has proved in his work.

l
a

Thou shalt lay stress discreetly upon elements within text.

6

Entice the reader to sample the delights of your text,
for what the Lord wants hidden can be full of pleasure.

HOLY Commandments are all very well and good for design beginners because, let's face it, they do work. The old saying is true: you need to learn the rules before you can break them. Once you have learnt the rules and can demonstrate that you can put them into practice, that's where the fun begins. It's just like being a child again: your parents teach you the rules but it's always far more fun breaking them! I'm sure even Joseph and **MARY** had their fair share of that when Jesus was a nipper; it's part of growing up. So why should typography be any different? First, you learn the rules, and later you delight in breaking them. You might make a complete mess, like when you covered the walls with paint when you were young and your **MOTHER** gave you a good hiding, but you learn from those mistakes and carry on breaking rules more successfully. It's hard work to break the rules and succeed, but it's better to fail in originality than to succeed in imitation. By sticking to Commandments, you are just copying other people's rules, so why not make your own? One **OF** the Fallen Angels, Michael Worthington, said: "True experimentation means taking risks. Not knowing the outcome but trying something that you think will be successful, but you have no proof. What happens if I mix element A with element F? Could be gold, could be sulphur." The age is upon us now when we have hardly any of the technical restraints that they had when the Commandments were rigidly practised. We have to thank such pioneers as Apple Computers, for designing the Macintosh, and such Fallen Angels as Rudy VanderLans and Zuzana Licko for buying one in 1984 and teaching us to experiment, try new and unusual things, and for **GOD**'s sake stop being so boring!

Thou shalt not use only capitals When setting vast body copy.

7

Do not forgo the liberal use of capitals within your text, for the geometric letterforms can provide some diabolically good outcomes.

JESUS CHRIST!

OK TRUE, ASCENDERS AND DESCENDERS DO HELP VIEWERS TO READ SLIGHTLY FASTER BUT

WHAT'S THE RUSH?

CAPITALS CAN BE A LOT MORE

POWERFUL

THAN LOWERCASE LETTERS MUCH

OF THE TIME ANYWAY.

AND IF THE ARTICLE IS ANY GOOD THERE WON'T

BE ANY PROBLEM AT ALL KEEPING

THE READER'S ATTENTION.

THINGS LIKE INCREASING LEADING CAN MAKE IT

EASIER TO READ.

THE TEXT MAY MAKE MORE OF A

DEMAND ON THE READER BUT

WHAT THE HELL

IS WRONG WITH THAT?

AS WELL AS AMUSING AND ENGAGING THE READER, TEXT TYPE CAN BE SET TO

DELIBERATELY

INFURIATE!

AND IF YOU'RE STILL

READING THIS

I BELIEVE THAT'S ALL THE PROOF YOU NEED THAT BODY COPY IS STILL

LEGIBLE AND

READABLE WHEN SET IN

UPPERCASE

AND THERE'S CERTAINLY NO

GODDAMN

LOSS OF INTEREST!

8

Thou shalt always align letters and words on a baseline.

The Lord designed letterforms to stand side by side, but there is no harm in their being lured away from each other.

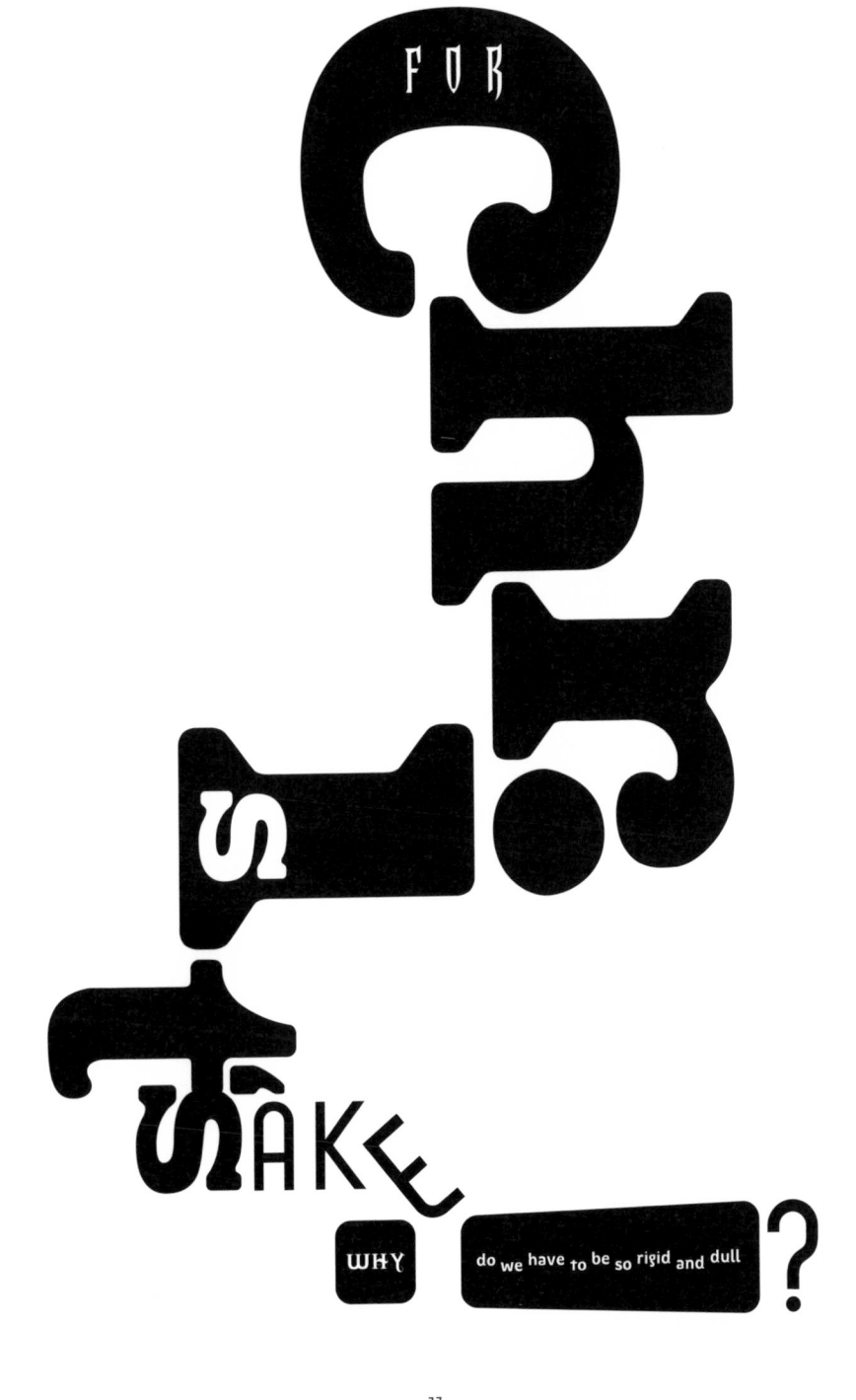

FOR Christ's SÂKE WHY do we have to be so rigid and dull?

6

Thou shalt use flush-left, ragged-right type alignment.

Yield to the temptation to align text in unusual ways.

> The account of Satan in the Bible implies that he turned
one third of the angelic host against God. It's not hard to imagine
that Satan went among the angels, seeking to
build support for his contention that they were far too good at
typography to stick to God's Commandments.

It was thus that Satan became filled
with violence against the rules.

Eventually Satan designed *Surfer*, a magazine that he must have felt
would deliver him to the position he believed should rightfully have
been his in the beginning. He decided to deceive his readers with the
psychological design of *Surfer* and by disobeying all God's express
Commandments.

Now Satan was more cunning than ever.
Through the design of *Surfer*, and later *Raygun*, he said to his readers that
God's almighty Commandments can successfully be broken.

He proved that once the rules are
broken, our eyes are opened to
endless typographic possibilities.
So when his readers saw that
Satan's design work was pleasant to the eye,
they too began to flout the rules.

Notice Satan's tactics: he didn't preach to his readers
directly, but instead his design did the talking and led
them to doubt God's laws.

IO

Thou shalt not make lines too short or too long.

Lure the reader down unfamiliar paths
by varying the length of your text.

Designers as entertainers...

The aim of expressive typography is to act as a engage them more?

vehicle for carrying a message.

Type should function as a means of

expression to the viewer as opposed to just being a transparent. Why not

Why not demand more of your readers?

God Help Us!

Normal
line
lengths
just
make
life
easier
for
the
reader.
Designers
spend
so
much
time
agonizing
over
their
work
that
it's
about
time
the
readers
put
some
effort
in
so
we
can
have
some
fun!

typographic hell